S0-BQE-716

only you

BY RICHARD KEHL

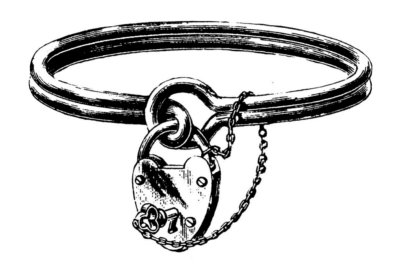

BLUE LANTERN BOOKS
MCMXCIV

COPYRIGHT © 1994, BLUE LANTERN STUDIO. ALL RIGHTS RESERVED.
FIRST PRINTING. PRINTED IN SINGAPORE THROUGH PALACE PRESS.
ISBN 1-883211-00-X

BLUE LANTERN BOOKS
PO BOX 4399 • SEATTLE, WASHINGTON • 98104-9996
TOLL FREE 1-800-354-0400

Let me not to the marriage of true minds
Admit impediments. Love is not love
Which alters when alteration finds,
Or bends with the remover to remove.
O, no! it is an ever fixed mark
That looks on tempests and is never shaken;
It is the star to every wand'ring bark,
Whose worth's unknown, although his height be taken.
Love's not Time's fool, though rosy lips and cheeks
Within his bending sickle's compass come;
Love alters not with his brief hours and weeks,
But bears it out even to the edge of doom.
    If this be error and upon me proved,
    I never writ, nor no man ever loved.

– William Shakespeare

PARIS
863

PICTURE CREDITS

Most of the unattributed illustrations in this book are within the public domain, or information about them was unavailable. Any omission of credit is thus inadvertent, and will be corrected in future printings if notification is sent to the publisher.